Praise for *Th...*

In Jan Seabaugh's stunning coll... we encounter a daughter documenting her mother's life and slippage into dementia with a degree of objectivity few could master. As Seabaugh remembers her mother, Vivian, as a young girl on the plains of South Dakota, or as a young wife with four small children, or even as a grieving widow, we encounter the complexity of family relationships where this collection of verse truly shines, for honesty and integrity direct the lens of Jan Seabaugh's poetry.

As she recalls, she also admits. As she remembers, she broadens the possible understanding of past events with newly occurring explanations not easily gained. As she states some hard lived truths, she also forgives. Few poets could deal with such emotional issues with the openness found in this collection. This acquaintanceship with Vivian Frame is heartwarming and heartbreaking and not to be missed.

Jessica Maich is the author of *The West End, Twenty-Four Questions for Billy,* and *Treatment Island.*

In this collection of poems about her mother's dementia, Jan Seabaugh remembers, "I pace to and fro with my lifeboat - my spiral notebook and pen." The reader of this volume by an accomplished poet will find both comfort and challenge in the author's lifeboat. Her unswerving aim throughout this this collection never wavers. From beginning to end, the reader is carefully and honestly led through the complex relationship of a mother and a daughter, as seen through the window of dementia. Jan Seabaugh has penned a volume which will find a lasting place in the heart of the reader.

Francis C. Gray, Retired Bishop in the Episcopal Church, Author of *My Day Job* and *Released*

These marvelous poems are narrative at their core. They trace nearly a hundred years of a woman becoming herself and defending that self against life's random interventions. Alongside these tales is another, even more compelling narrative: a daughter's struggle toward her own selfhood as she deals with the mother of memory and the mother who now needs her physical care. Jan Seabaugh's crisp and precise detail pulls the reader into these poems and convinces us that ultimately this is a story of love.

Sonia Gernes, Professor Emerita of English, University of Notre Dame, and the author of *The Way to St. Ives* and five books of poetry

the sheep at the top of the stairs

JAN SEABAUGH

Viveca Smith Publishing
McKinney, Texas

Copyright 2023 Jan Seabaugh

All rights reserved. No part of this publication may be reproduced without written permission from Viveca Smith Publishing except for brief quotations for articles and reviews.

ISBN: 978-1-7327568-3-0

Library of Congress Control Number: 2022950693

for my mother
Vivian Carol Frame

January 15, 1919-
June 3, 2020

Vivian and her mother, Agnes Thurn, 1920

Contents

Home 1
The Dad Museum 4
32 Years After the Fact 6
Dementia 12
Thanksgiving Before Closing 15
Some Bright Morning 17
Dementia and the Baby Monkey 20
The Little Engine That Could 23
My Dark Ages 25
The Widow Show 27
Nobody Home: Second Childhood 31
The Mockery of Old Age 33
Alzheimer's Whispering 34
Rituals of Morning 36
Return Trip 38
Talking in My Sleep 41
The Afterlife 43
Islands 45
The Night I Tell Her 48
At the Audiologist's 51
The Others 53
Special Delivery 56

Peace, in Pieces	59
Fresh Air	61
Before and After	66
Mothers and Daughters	67
After Visiting My Mother	70
Beyond Belief: The Churchgoer	71
Today	74
What Goes Without Saying	76
Mom's Birthday Surprise	78
Dementia and/or My Mother	80
The Citizen	82
Memory Loss	87
A Fantasy of La-la Land	90
Her Childbearing Years	92
Cruelty	94
Cruelty II	96
The Inadequacies of Pig Latin	98
Envoy	100
June 3, 2020	105
A Time and Place to Mourn	107
My Travel Companion	109
In Closing	112

Home

"Last night I dreamed,"
my mother tells me
somewhat angrily,
"that there was a sheep
at the top of the stairs."

She is twitching back and forth
in her green corduroy rocker,
the stairs in question leading up
behind her to the landing.
It will be her last summer in her own house.
By now the furniture is furred with dust
she can no longer see, and the mice
make brazen crossings of the parquet floor.
Even in dereliction, though, the place
is what she once would have called
"high off the hog."

At seventeen, my mother left the ranch
where she had grown up in the saddle,
tending herds of "stupid stupid" sheep,
so that she could get a college education,

*wear smart suits and heels to work each day,
drink water from a tap, wash clothes
and bathe without lugging buckets.
She wanted central heating—not a stove
that needed constant feeding with wood
or cow chips, its meager warmth shared
with bum lambs and sick animals in the kitchen.
No, she was determined to "get out of there!"*

*And she did. She left western South Dakota
behind—her parents, the rattlers, the house
whose west-facing windows had once all been
busted out by hail, the fields where
grasshoppers had come like a dark cloud
and stripped away months of work,
where dust storms had come and left
everything black, a half-inch deep on the sills,
where there were so many funerals for children
she hated the smell of flowers all her life.*

*"Out home" there had been hardship.
"Out home" nobody had anything,
so nobody looked down on the poor.
"Out home" everyone went out picking
buffaloberries and chokecherries in summer.*

*And on this humid August afternoon,
coming into the house after her third trip
out to the clothesline, she uses the words again:
"Out home," she tells me peevishly,*

*"you could hang out the wash
and in twenty minutes it would be dry."*

*Now that her memory is retreating,
and she is being forced to give up the house,
will she find herself, after all, back on that ranch?*

*She dreamed last night of sheep.
Where would they be leading their shepherdess,
if not home?*

The Dad Museum

My mother's eyes are failing.
Dust collects on the curling Polaroids
jammed into the picture frames,
on the Navajo rugs, on the napkin ring
from the supply ship that my father
served on during the war.
Still, she holds on to the role of curator.

Aside from the decay she cannot see,
she has preserved everything exactly as it was.
No wall has been painted a different color;
not a piece of furniture has been moved—
not even the bedside table in the living room,
which he lugged downstairs temporarily
back in 1969 to support the new stereo,
mute now for a third of a century.
In the garage, his workbench presents the tableau
of the last time he ever changed his oil—
a wrench, a funnel, a stained plastic pan—
while the vise gapes open, slack and still,
as if locked in its last breath.

In the August of his passing, the fireplace was empty,
and it has remained empty ever since,
even when the power went out for five days
in a bitter February, and her neighbors waded through the snow
to see whether or not she was still alive.
Meanwhile, the firewood he had stacked for the winters
gradually rotted, dissolved back into the earth.
She would rather be cold, she told her visitors,
than light a fire and have to deal with the ashes.

But now things have become too much for her.
"This house!" she moans. "What a nightmare!"—
the antiquated well pump, the termites,
the downed trees, the stove with its two burners out,
the driveway impassable in rains.
She never liked the place to begin with;
she wanted a big sunny kitchen, she'd told him,
wall to wall carpet, central air,
a manageable yard, no stairs to climb,
walking distance to the store and library,
a small place they could grow old in together—
nothing like this.

But now she won't consider moving, no.
Arms folded, she refuses to abandon all this
for an easier life in her remaining years.

"This is where I lived with your dad,"
she tells us firmly. "This is where
I want to die."

32 Years After the Fact

8 am

As soon as I come down for coffee,
my mother takes up the subject:

You know, maybe it was all those chest x-rays
they used to give the engineers every year.
Of course at that time it was TB
the company was worried about.
They thought it was *good* they were doing.

Or it could be he just absorbed something
from working around electronics his whole life—
the radar and radio transmitters and televisions,
those big antennas out in the desert,
or the equipment he built for those satellites
to send pictures back from the moon.
Who knows what all that really does to the body?
But he was doing what he loved.

Maybe, though, his lungs were damaged early on
by that flu that killed so many in 1918.

You know his folks really thought
they'd lost him then.
The doctor rode out to the ranch
but told them there was nothing he could do.
Imagine those poor young parents
out there alone with that sick baby!
Still, your dad pulled through that somehow.
But it could have left him vulnerable.

1 pm

After lunch I am sitting in what had been his chair.
She pushes away her empty plate and sighs:

But I suppose it was all those years of smoking—
let's face it, that's the biggie—
all those cartons of Lucky Strikes and Kents—
so much smoke you couldn't see across the room.
And they used to tell us the filters made them safe. Ha.
What a bunch of criminals.

And it was only after he quit that he started
putting on all those extra pounds.
When we were growing up, we *wanted* calories—
everybody was just trying to get enough,
but now they say there's an obesity epidemic.
Your dad never got what you'd call obese,
but maybe his weight had something to do with it;
he had always been so healthy before.

Of course, food used to be real food.
Maybe it was something they started
giving the cattle—God knows what;
your dad did love his steaks.
And I just read in the Post that grilling them
on that Smoky Joe of his was probably the worst.

They are on and on about diet now.
But I never liked to put things on the table
that your dad didn't like—broccoli or carrots,
things they now say are so good for you.
And some foods they recommend these days
your dad and I never even saw as kids—
most things just didn't grow well out there.

3 pm

Walking back up the long driveway to the house
after getting the mail, she resumes:

But then living out here in those last years
couldn't have been good for him, either—
that long commute in Beltway traffic.
We could move closer, I used to tell him,
have more time together, not so much driving.
But he loved this place.

Or it might have been from something as stupid
as those chemicals he used to spread on the lawn.

Remember? He was set on growing that bluegrass
even though our soil wasn't right for it.
Still, he did so enjoy a beautiful yard.

7:05 pm

After the news, she checks the potatoes, says
they need a few more minutes, and then:

Or it could go way back to when he was in CCCs
and they were putting out those forest fires
in the Black Hills, the smoke he inhaled then,
or some sort of chemicals they were spraying.

Of course they say now that those Navy ships
like he was on were just filled with asbestos.
Or maybe he was exposed to something
when he was stationed in Japan
after the surrender—some radioactivity
left over from the bombs,
or toxins that got released in the fires.
He never really talked about what it was like over there.
After the war, everybody just wanted to move on.

10:45 pm

My mother has made us each a bourbon and Coke,
which had always been *his* drink, his rare nightcap,
while in those days she had no stomach for alcohol.

Gazing at the empty fireplace now,
she revives the subject yet again:

But maybe it was just something he was born with.
His folks both lived into their nineties, though,
and they had no history of cancer on either side.
His brothers all smoke, so why him?

I dated lots of nice guys in high school and college,
but it never crossed my mind to marry any one of them.
When I met your dad, though, I just *knew*.
This was during the war, of course,
and the Navy wouldn't let anybody
who wasn't single remain in radar school.
So we waited until the day he graduated,
then walked straight from the ceremony
to the minister's house and said our vows.

We didn't have very long together
before he was shipped out, though,
and then—egad—there was all that uncertainty.
I moved back with my folks when I was pregnant
and stayed out there on the ranch
until your dad was discharged from the service.
By that time Elaine was already walking,
and right away he had to find work and a place to live,
and we were just trying to make ends meet.
He started putting in those long hours at the plant,
working nights, too, repairing TVs,
and then the rest of you kids came along.

It was just busy busy busy for years and years.
But we thought we had finally made it;
we had just gotten the last of you kids through school
and were finally looking forward to some time to ourselves.
And then—

She shakes her head:
I just can't figure it out.

Dementia

First, things began to go missing,
swept overboard off the top deck.
Anything not already deep in the hold,
securely stowed, was washed away.
Things set aboard in the morning
disappeared by evening—
the preceding chapter of a book,
the answer to a repeated question,
the operating instructions for the new oven.
But we did not fret those petty losses.
Though at sea in such moments,
my mother still could sail.

But now the leaks have multiplied,
stealing in through every seam.
Alarmed, I hover around her
with my spiral notebook and pen.

What do you save from a sinking ship?
First the people: her mom and dad,
she making bread on Saturday mornings,
loaves enough to last the week,

playing piano for church and silent films;
he as a child racing around on the deck
while his seasick parents hung over the rail
during the rough Atlantic crossing
that brought them to this country,
then as a homesteader chasing after the horse
on which he had placed, bareback, his tiny daughter;
her little brother with his adorable curls,
later a pilot in the Berlin airlift, a daredevil,
one reason she was too anxious to fly;
her father's parents, who never learned English,
with whom she could never converse;
her other grandparents, who once sent the gift
of a windmill, because pumping water
for all the livestock and the house
from that deep artesian well was such a chore,
and oh, what a difference that made.
Next save the animals: the saddle horses
Dick and then Lady, and the team, Prince and Star,
the dog Nippy and cats Whitey and Old Black Joe,
and Felix, the maimed cat she rescued after the owner
of the hardware store shot him for stealing chicks;
even the bargain goat that her dad paid a dollar for
and that enjoyed making an unholy clatter
on the corrugated metal of the dipping pen.

She used to tell stories as though
laying up preserves to nourish us forever,
but we never thought we would need them.
How careless we were with her life!

The memories she would recount so often
that we would roll our eyes at the supper table
now lie in fragments, half-submerged.
What exactly was the disgrace of the Hofzinger girls?
As for the tragedy of the little Hungarian man
who repaired their shoes—how did her father find him?
And who paid for the funeral when the church
took the money but refused to bury him?
What was the name of the family friend
who accidentally drove over her father
when he got out to open a cattle gate?
How did she and her mother kill the rattlesnake?
How many grades did she teach in the country school?
Who was it that introduced her to my father?
All too often, trying to salvage everything,
I resort to point-blank questions:
"How did that story go?"
"Who was that person?"
But then she grimly replies:
"I don't remember."

Treasures once recorded so clearly on the manifest
are now drifting into the deep.
My mother's eyes, though, glitter with valor—
like a captain still gripping the helm,
preparing to go down with the ship.

Thanksgiving Before Closing

Selling our mother's house
on a bright blue autumn morning
over the holiday,
my sister and I are standing
with potential buyers
in the back yard by the well
when a gust sends down a shower
of golden leaves from the poplars.

The conversation stops;
the wife says
Ah!—
and looking up,
stretches out her hands,
palms skyward.

A month from now we will sign the official papers,
passing them around a bank table
to close the sale of the property.
I will detach the house key from the chain

bearing the name tag "Vivian,"
handing it over to them,
locking my mother out
of her own house for good.

But this is the morning
of the real changing of hands—
when the spirit of the place
approves the new inhabitants
with the flying colors
of beautiful, dying leaves.

Some Bright Morning

Waking up, I see my mother's bed empty across the hall
and know she has been wandering in the night again.
I hear her voice in the predawn stillness,
harshly calling, "Where *are* you?"
I find her downstairs in our dark guest room,
chilled and grim, rocking in a hard chair.
After a trip to the bathroom in the wee hours,
she could not find her way back to bed,
though she has lived here now for four years.
"Well," I say, "we may as well have a cup of coffee."

When I used to visit my mother's house,
I would wake up on summer mornings
in what had been my sister's bed,
in a room painted blue fifty years before.
The window would be open; the air, dense
with Virginia green and textured with birdsong,
would breathe on the white curtains,
where shadows swayed as if treading water.
I would hear my mother downstairs,
with the radio tuned to the morning news,

opening more windows and turning on the fan
to let in the coolness before the heat of the day.

Of all those mornings at her house
there was a last one. There had to be.
By then she had taken to wiping dishes
with water she heated in a saucepan on the stove
as if back on the homestead on the prairie.
She kept bringing in the daily paper
although by then too blind to read it.
Her car had a smashed fender
she was at a loss to explain.

I remember coming down
and waiting in her kitchen
for what turned out to be
the last breakfast she would ever make,
watching as she spooned bacon grease
from a jelly jar into the skillet
she had used every day of my life.
She set out two poorly washed plates,
the sunlight flashing gold
from the traces of eggs
left from mornings gone by.

Now she is sitting with me in my own kitchen,
drinking her coffee as the sun rises;
it lights up the salt and pepper shakers,
causes glints to veer around the room
whenever we lift and lower our cups.

It looks for all the world like glory,
though we are just two women in pajamas,
silently sharing buttered toast—

perhaps a scene I will remember
some other bright morning
like, but so unlike, this.

Dementia and the Baby Monkey

Sometimes, now that all the pleases
and thank-yous and soft words
of fond memory are wearing away,
the armature emerges from underneath
the whole cloth of my mom, and
I glimpse again the wire mother.
She sits disengaged, vacant,
not seeming to realize that the object
that is with her, her child, is alive.

I remember this mother, too,
and then it becomes easy to forget
the character of happiness:
the breakfasts at little cafes
on cross-country jaunts;
the first morning of first grade
walking to school along the railroad tracks,
my hand in hers, me in my new plaid dress;
long evenings when she sat with a crossword
while my dad read the *Electronic News*;
and all the recipes and newspaper clippings

labeled "Thought you'd enjoy!"
sent over fifty years.

No, on a too-long afternoon of dementia,
when she is silent, and I feel unwitnessed,
attentions unpaid to me long ago throb again:
the young mother behind the newspaper,
shrouded in cigarette smoke, invisible
but for an anxious foot, ominous, jiggling;
or hour after hour of her facing away from me
while she hung clothes, scrubbed pans,
ironed shirts, fried potatoes, paid bills,
even played piano—and better her back to me
than were I to interrupt and make her turn,
her eyes glittering with the ferocious expression
of a bust of Beethoven as she snapped,
"What do you want?" in such a tone of voice
that I could not possibly want anything,
could not lift my paper with its good grade
that my teacher had assured me
my mother would be so proud of,
could not, later on, tell her that my body was changing,
could not expose to her my fantasy of mattering.
And how could I want to add weight
to that chain of one darn thing after another
she so often called her life?

Life. She sits here now, rocking,
her tired head bent to her chest as if praying.
It has been so long since I heard her really laugh.
Her body has grown soft over the years,
its wiry tension gone.
How human, after all, we both became.

The Little Engine That Could

Our mother's version would have been quite different.
My sisters and I used to laugh about it:
The Little Engine That Bit Off More Than It Could Chew,
The Little Engine That Had Got In Over Its Head,
The Little Engine That Was Too Big For Its Britches.

She could have made it a real send-up,
the engine—let's call it "missy"—sliding backwards
while chuffing away with its self-affirmations—
thought balloons drifting up to the top of the page
while defeats mount up at the base of the mountain.

No sense people flapping their gums,
she would say: either you can or you can't,
so you'd better just see to it that you can.
Nevertheless, I secretly admired
the little engine that fueled itself on hope.

She had always said that life was one step forward
and two steps back; and now, I confess, it's true:
every day on the steep grade of her old age,

she loses ground; her powers fail:
sight, hearing, memory, cognition, speech.

She is no longer capable of saying
I told you so, but I will myself concede
that dementia is not a hill to be surmounted
by positive visualization and a persistent will.
If you cannot think, how can you think you can?

But if the moral of the story is about not giving up
in the face of challenges, my mother, pessimist
though she was, is its hero every day.
Like a heart, drumming steadily in its darkness,
never having to be told or cajoled to beat,

she keeps on going, even in winter,
head down, hood up, eyes watering,
rattling her walker across the parking lot
with me into the Target, where in bad weather
we take our daily constitutional indoors—

just because—thanks to our lucky stars
and not ourselves—we still can.

My Dark Ages

In the darkness of my closet behind the dolls
I kept an educational booklet about foreign lands,
because of two images that, at twelve years old, I loved.

One was of a woman with dark hair smiling into bright sunlight
in a colorful ruffled dress and a hat piled high with fruit.
She was set against a background of green leaves,
as though she had just flowered directly from the foliage.
She was like no one I knew or could ever become,
holding herself as frankly and loosely and proudly as a tree.

The second photo from the montage showed a parade
in a sunny plaza, people holding aloft a straight chair
with a seated statue of a woman and a baby,
both decorated as richly as fancy cakes.
The crowd was conspicuously happy.
Unlike in street scenes on our nightly news,
nobody was throwing stones
or setting themselves or buildings afire,
no police were clubbing black fathers, and
no demonstrators were holding signs,
their faces distorted by shouting.

What would it be like to live flagrantly in a celebrating world,
wearing loud clothes, being gaudy, dancing in public,
laughing without a hand in front of one's mouth?
I visited the photos privately, like icons—
not sacred in the way of, say, the justices of the Supreme Court,
or thrift, or the dictionary, but sacred to me as a mystery.

One Friday afternoon (cleaning day)
I got up the courage to reveal these treasures
to my mother—wordlessly, reverently, timidly.
Our living room smelled of the vacuum.
She paused long enough from dusting
to scowl and say, "Judas Priest.
The Dark Ages are alive and well
in the twentieth century."

The Widow Show

That is what part of me thought of it all:
my mother's shaky walk to the open casket
with her four grown children,
two on each side, arm in arm;
her repeated declarations
that she envied the women in India,
who were allowed to commit *suttee*
rather than prolong their misery;
her claims to be unable to sleep without him,
when on visits home I could see for myself
that she lay on her side of their double bed,
book face-down on her chest, snoring.

That part of me suspected a crime—
as if my father's death had been caused
not by cigarettes or the tobacco companies,
but by her, her flood of words and thoughts,
filling his lungs so that he could not surface,
could not take a single breath
that she had not breathed already—
suffocating his spirit, or perhaps
driving his body to suicide by cancer.

And then she lamented that he had been
the love of her life! What theater!

And at twenty-four I hated drama,
preferring instead a self-contained manner,
seemly, efficient, and absolutely faithful
not only to the memory of my father
as a real living person, but also
to whoever he had secretly been within,
whoever he might have wanted to become
had it not been for her, for all of us.

But how could I maintain a policy
of keeping myself to myself
when my mother did not
keep herself to herself, but performed
all these posturings to death! Death!

I wore a bright yellow dress that day
to signify that no, it was not this corpse
that I would honor and remember, but him,
and that I would always, always stay the girl
whose dad was still alive in her life.

Today he would have been
one hundred two years old.
My mother does not realize.
Spring has come again,
with its same old lilies-of-the-valley,

its perennially fragrant peonies,
its birthday without candles,
without his breath to wish with.
I grant now that he is dead.
My mother sips ginger ale
through a paper straw.

I think of her now as she was then,
younger than I am now;
I think of myself that day in the funeral home,
the part of me that was so prim and haughty
and offended by her display of grief—

Yet now it appears she had fully realized
how final that goodbye would turn out to be—
down to each familiar finger on his chest;
and now I can believe in a sincere wish
to just call a halt right then and there
and declare the life that she'd had *enough*;
and now her physical exhaustion looks credible,
her insomnia when no one else was in the house,
her body too alarmed by loneliness to rest.

I think of that last time I saw him,
and of that part of me that felt
so painfully, proudly sensitive to truth,
of my mother crossing that threshold
into that new reality in which
I refused to participate.

So what did the widow show that day?
Was it something not genuine?
Was it, after all, me—the part of me
that was so unbending, so resistant
to experiencing grief as to declare it
false? For that has turned into the truest,
sorriest, saddest, softest part,
the portion I try to give my mother now,
now that it is mostly too late,
on this May day, having ginger ale,
when I am fully present, but she
in her dementia, is so absent,
having survived not only my father,
but even herself, the grieving widow
that alas, she really was.

Nobody Home: Second Childhood

One afternoon nearly a decade ago,
my mother looked up from a letter
reporting the death of a girlhood friend
and calmly announced,
"Now there is nobody left
who remembers me when I was young."

This was before the dementia moved in
and swept away her adult self,
piece and piece, into a sea of oblivion
reaching further and further back in her life.
Now she is as if standing on an island,
the familiar dry ground of her childhood,
just beyond the box elders and the windmill,
there by the hand-cranked cream separator,
all alone. For there is nobody left
to remember her when she was young.

Sometimes she appears to me
like a little girl lost among strangers.
And then I imagine the grown-ups
in whom she had placed her childhood trust,

those whom she now might still find familiar,
locked as they are in death, frantic with pity—
her mother and grandparents,
all dead before I was born,
her father with his cowboy hat,
bolo tie, and Lawrence Welk accent.
So I try to proxy for them, their touch,
their songs, their ways of saying and soothing,
but I can only guess at them, at their sense of her,
as if I remembered her when she was young.

Then when as a joke one day I sit
sideways on the recliner
across my mother's lap,
like an enormous baby, she laughs
and put her arms around me—

as if she remembers
me when I was young.

The Mockery of Old Age

Sometimes, when my mother is toddling
hurriedly to the bathroom
with her hands fluttering at her waistband,
or lowering her whole head
with extended tongue
toward a spoonful of food,
I find myself inadvertently
mirroring her—
putting my body in her place
to feel for myself what it is like
to be that old.
She does not see me do this.

But sometimes after drifting off to sleep in a chair,
her head bent completely
to the buttons of her blouse,
she lifts just her eyes to meet mine.
"Look," her taunting gaze seems to tell me.
"One day this will be you."

Alzheimer's Whispering

Since dementia enclosed my mother,
I sometimes find myself seeking her recognition
the way that, as a child on a field trip to the zoo,
I would stand outside the cage of some exotic animal,
hoping that from all the visitors gathered at the bars,
I alone would be singled out as special.

Back then I wanted the eyes of the tigress or polar bear,
sweeping idly over our faces, to lock upon mine,
surprised—for here at last was a kindred spirit come!—
a human able to communicate telepathically,
a fellow animal worth emerging from the cave to meet.
I would become the zebra's best friend!
I would be able to comprehend the llama's thoughts!

Now as my mother sits next to me at the table,
she reaches for a straw and takes a sip—
recalling to my mind a panda I once watched
pull to its mouth slantwise a bamboo shoot,
oblivious to all the spectators, including me.

I shake off this association with a laugh.
But seeing me laugh, my mother laughs, too,
as if she, with uncanny understanding,
proved our real connection for my sake.

Rituals of Morning

When I saw my mother
lying asleep this morning,
I thought, Oh, please,
please—don't wake up just yet.
Let me have this time to myself.
I am not ready to play cards again,
to utter words that vanish
like pebbles into the face of the ocean,
or to sit in silence with you another day
in the solitary confinement of your old age.

But then she looked too still.

Instantly, countless other mornings
came springing forth from their dormancies—
my mother her pre-dementia self again,
walking up her long gravel driveway under the poplars
reading the front page of the *Washington Post*,
pausing to pluck dead leaves off a geranium
she'd planted in an old Maxwell House can;

then after finishing the paper,
while the light was still young,
sitting with her coffee at her dining room table,
writing letters to us in a beautiful hand—

all these scenes rushing in review
while I approached her bedside,
before I could see her pajamas subtly moving,
or the flushed pinkness of her living face.

And then I backed away
with my hand over my heart,
like someone who has very nearly escaped
death—this moment casting its shadow
over the long hours I would wind up,
after all, having my coffee alone.

Return Trip

As parents my mother and father were best
in the front seat of a Chrysler, in summer,
the four of us in the back, riding in silence.
We would be out on the open road.
The first day, we would still be encased
in the personalities we had constructed
over the past school year,
but by the time we crossed the Mississippi,
we would become our old selves again.

Gradually we would regain the ability
to see outside our own thoughts—
at a man walking up a dirt driveway
from the road to a white house, carrying his mail;
a deer glancing up from the edge of a woods;
silos of corrugated metal, swimming with heat;
fields with their rows on swift parade;
a gas station attendant sitting with his dog;
a mountain with snow on top,
dark green up to the tree line,

with a paler vertical stripe
marking the firebreak.

Life would recover its beloved immensity;
the roads could go everywhere again.

Right now my own town looks like someplace
we might have ridden through on vacation—
a slow tree-lined street in the Midwest,
dusk bringing with it smells of suppers,
sprinklers twirling in the yards,
lights coming on in kitchen windows,
kids calling to one another,
"Invisible man on first!" "Untimes!"
As a child, I would have wondered,
What would it be like to live here?
What is that woman in her yard thinking?
And now I do live here, and now
I am that woman in her yard, thinking:

One time when we stopped for gas
I came out of the restroom and saw my mother
in a green cotton dress and summer sandals,
her white purse dangling from her forearm,
squatting in a drainage ditch
alongside the filling station,
panning for gold.

My father was standing by the car,
smiling at her for being so exactly herself.

Now she is sitting beside me
in a lawn chair by the peonies.
She looks complete, all gathered-in,
as if she has actually arrived
at wherever it was we had always been going.
A firefly lights and goes dark behind her.
A car goes by with me inside.

Talking in My Sleep

In my dreams, she can speak again.

In one she stares out a window,
thumbs forward on her hips,
musing aloud: "I wonder
whatever happened
to the Hawley girl."

In another it is raining.
She comes in off the porch,
shaking out her red jacket,
unfolding the damp newspaper
she has brought up from the street.
"Nice weather for ducks," she remarks.

In the one most recent, it is night.
The late news is over;
it is time to be turning in.
She claps her two palms down
onto the arms of her green corduroy chair
and says, "Well. I think I'll go up."

She walks her glass to the sink
and turns out the light in the kitchen.
Only after she has climbed the stairs
will it dawn on my sleeping self
that all this has been a miracle:
my mother back to her everyday self,
the voice unmistakably hers.

And I wake up amazed
at the true miracle
beneath the dreamed one:
somehow my mother is still living
in me, exactly as she was.

The Afterlife

In my Father's house are many mansions…
I go to prepare a place for you.
— *John 14:2*

Maybe even now He is preparing a place
for my mother to live forever—
I imagine Him tending to the details:
He is putting the light back into the stars
so they can shine on her the way they did
that night she sat on the hood of the car
after the dance and talked until dawn.
He has found the satin blue-gray dress she wore
and fixed the zipper, which would come off track
a decade later, right before the company party.
He has reassembled her uncle's Model A
so that her cousin can get her there in time,
and He has put the pine trees back together
that once lined that road into the Hills.
He is restoring to her my father in full health.
He has set her house back up on the ranch,
rewired the fencing, brought back all the sheep,
and put the barn and windmill in their places.

He has woken up her father and mother
from their long sleep—her little brother, too—
and summoned them to the table before her.
He has set a jar of buffaloberry jelly on the sill
and her white cat on the warm boards on the step.
He has led her horse, Lady, back into the meadow.
And He has not forgotten her, herself,
recollecting every breath she took that day,
and every day, the limber fleetness of her legs,
the warmth of her hands and feet,
and that old clarity of sight and sound.
He has kept a perfect schedule of her pulse,
so that her heart can do it all again,
racing and aching and breaking whenever it should.
Even the sequential order of her eggs,
month by month, and their instants of release,
He has memorized forever, so that she can expect
me, and my brother and sisters, to join her
at our proper moments, and all of us can be together.
But given that He is not ready for her just yet,
this moment, too, must be taking shape in eternity—
now, as she drifts in and out by a snowy window,
and I watch her half-asleep in my own house
of only imperfect, only human understanding.

Islands

Once when still a teenager at home,
I was watching TV with my mother—
she in one green chair, I in the other.
Our program was ending with inspiring music,
panoramic views, and a voice intoning,

"No man is an island…"

At that point my mother turned to me
with an unexpectedly hostile look
and declared, "What a bunch of hooey!"
We all are islands!
What we need are bridges!"

Her words struck my warm oceanic feelings
like a cold wave of literal ocean—
hard, powerful, and full of grit.
But I did not think to ask my mother,
What makes a bridge?

I held on to that poetry of faith in common ground,
concealed, solid, deep beneath apparent separations;
she, though, spent hours talking to my siblings and me—
unbroken chains of memories, judgments, facts, worries—
as if casting out grappling hooks for a surface boarding.

But we tended to draw ourselves to ourselves,
her eloquent sentences sinking into our silences
like rain into the sea. The more we withdrew,
the more she talked; the more she talked,
the more we withdrew.

And so it was that after our father's death,
we became not so much a family
as an archipelago of remote private sanctuaries.
One could still tell, though, how we might once
have fit together, like the continents on a globe.

Right now my mother is sitting in her chair,
and I in mine. She is submerged in her dementia.
It has been six years since I brought her home with me.
She who once spoke so tirelessly, no longer speaks at all.
If language had ever made a bridge, it is washed away.

I have grown so used to whatever lay between us—
that impasse, like the space between repelling magnets—
that today, when I wordlessly take her hands and feel
her skin in contact, all at once real and alive to me,
our human electricity passing unimpeded in between,

I physically startle, as if a bird had flown
straight through a window I had believed closed.
But it's the truth: here we are together, she and I,
in our two chairs like two boats on the carpet,
or perhaps like two turtles from opposite shores

finally meeting nose to nose on the sea floor.

The Night I Tell Her

In our house
nobody spoke of
love.

I first heard the word
applied to me
in high school
by a teenaged boy.

There was a time, though,
one evening in the late sixties,
when something on the news
sent my mother over the edge,
and she pronounced the word many times,
loudly, in anger.

"Love love love love!" she mocked.
"There's all this hippie talk of love,
and they don't even know what it is!"
And then, as if to inform those
goofball flower children on TV, she declared:
"Love is what happens between a man and a woman."

Now she is ninety-six years old,
and the man who was all that to her
has been gone for nearly forty years,
his cancer meanwhile disproving
to her, once and for all,
the supposed love of God.

So here we are, she and I, tonight.
I have filled her hot water bottle
and slipped it into its little case,
a Fair Isle turtleneck knitted by my sister;
and laid out on her bed her cozy pajamas,
a Christmas gift from my brother,
with the ultrathick treaded socks
another sister sent
to warm her ever-cold feet;
and turned on the desk lamp
so that she can find her way
to the bathroom in the dark.

After climbing under the covers
with her "warm baby" in its little sweater,
she reaches up to me with her right arm,
meaning, "Give me a hug."

In our house
we still do not speak of
love.

Leaning down to say good night, though,
with my mother's arm crooked around my neck
in our bedtime routine, I ask myself,
"What, then, is all of this?"

At the Audiologist's

Today I am taking my mother
to get her hearing aids.
She rides along in silence;
I remind her four times where we are going.

Her talk once flowed through our lives
like a great river, sweeping along everything
she saw, thought, read, or recalled—
the voting records of those rascals in Washington,
the flakiness and divorces of family outliers,
the unaccountable rituals of Catholics and other religionists,
the swarms of grasshoppers that darkened the sun in the thirties,
the need to identify the gene that causes criminality,
the biographical details of the presidents
(including James Polk, who as a boy underwent surgery
for urinary stones through an incision behind the scrotum,
and without anesthesia, can you imagine?!),
the different personalities of her family's two saddle horses,
the constantly disorganized purses of her friends,
who could never find their keys.

Not long ago on her best days
she could still ask me, over and over,
"Are your boys married?"
In the wedding photos she stands at the altar,
wearing a blue dress and a vacant expression.

Now she sits with me in a soundproof booth
wearing headphones, through which
the audiologist behind the glass
is apparently telling her, Repeat after me.

At first I see his lips move
without any response from her.
He turns knobs, watches, tries again.
Again. Finally I hear it:
the long-lost voice of my own mother.
She caressingly repeats each word
from her old and beautiful and familiar vocabulary:
daybreak playground birthday hardware iceberg eardrum.
Her face comes to attention, staring into space
as if seeing someone she almost recognizes.
I could listen to her forever; it is like a cradle rocking:
cowboy drawbridge stairway grandson farewell.

The Others

I see them in produce aisles,
taking directions to a particular apple, or
overloudly justifying the ethics
of detaching two perfect bananas
from a too-large bunch.

I see them outside the mall,
lifting wheelchairs from their trunks,
in hospital corridors,
walking alongside with an IV pole,
or in the large-print sections
of public libraries,
holding out books
and shouting into the quiet,
"Have you read this one?"

I see them in restaurants,
their own plates long clean,
watching, repeating, "I know,
but you can take the rest home."
I see them in drug stores

helping search a packed wallet
for the right insurance card,
or carrying two plastic packages
of adult women's diapers, or
in the greeting card aisle,
displaying options one by one,
reciting each text aloud.

I see them in doctors' waiting rooms
holding the clipboard and office pen,
leaning in to explain: "They want you
to rate your pain level from one to ten,"
then sharing photos from the magazines—
a baby, a hummingbird cake, and look,
a blue hydrangea.

I see them in pews at church,
their heads jerking up from silent prayer
when the voice next to them declares,
"This headset is worthless!
I can't hear a damn thing!"
And I see them sometimes
in parking lots, their cars parallel
to mine, standing, like me,
beside an open passenger door,
hands stretched out to assist, waiting,
and like fellow citizens who cross paths
in a foreign land, who recognize one another

as sharers of a certain kind of life,
we exchange respectful nods, then continue
our forays in this larger world,
steadying an elbow, adjusting a sweater,
seeing, and seen.

Special Delivery

I dream that we are at my mother's old house.
It is the present, though—she deep in her silence,
her loss of initiative, her dementia.
I go upstairs to move some heavy furniture,
leaving her for the moment in her corduroy chair.

But when I glance out the window, there she is,
walking down the long gravel driveway to the mailbox.
She has somehow managed, all by herself,
to put on her red jacket with its red hood.
She is holding what appears to be a letter.

Before she reaches the street, I come running up.
She is clutching tight a battered envelope
bearing the name of her firstborn in shaky script.
Inside is a card, weighty and beautiful,
dense with affection, gratitude, fullness of heart.

My mother looks at me urgently, mutely.
The letter has no valid stamp, no street address.
"Do you want Elaine to get this?" I loudly ask.

She nods. How she has summoned all her forces
to do this—like a mother lifting a car off a baby!

I promise that I will deliver her message.
Awake, I feel no less bound to keep that pledge,
to make certain that my sister receives the love
my mother was so desperate to convey
she burrowed a channel through my dreams.

But Elaine has long felt rejected by our mother
as a broken thing in need of fixing, of thwarting.
And no doubt our mother felt rejected in her turn,
as a source of childhood suffering, a polar opposite,
a relentless critic, an incompatible wavelength.

Yet they made their trips to see the trilliums in bloom,
exchanged sheet music and recipes, played Scrabble;
Elaine brought fresh peaches and homemade pastries,
included our mother in holidays and vacations,
nursed her for weeks after she broke her ankle.

It's too late for that heartfelt correspondence,
but early this morning I send my dream to Elaine,
and then all day I check my inbox for an answer,
one side of my heart waiting for the other,
its valves agape like the mouths of baby birds.

And although my mother looks blank today,
with no sign of having anything to communicate,
I sense the sender of the dream still on the wing
between my flesh and blood and my flesh and blood.
Several days pass before my sister writes at last:

"That dream you had…it kind of got to me."

Peace, in Pieces

Sometimes I speak of him aloud,
pausing the walker alongside the river:
"Smile now, I will text a photo of you
to Mark, he will like that" or
"Mark wrote that the eye of the hurricane
passed just east of them."

My mother's eyes come to attention then,
the pupils drawn forward like needles
magnetized by the name of her only son.
She who has been so lost to herself
has not lost her feeling for him;
I can see a small light left on inside.

My brother's memory has suffered, too,
but with a different remembering,
a different forgetting.
What hell now separates him
from his home and his boyhood self,
the sensitive, buoyant teenager
sent to war fifty years ago?
What survived what was survived?

He had been the magic in the house.
Every family, like even the most
perfectly assembled kite,
needs a lifting breeze like him.

A year goes by, two, three.
Every now and again
a card, a text, a tin of fudge arrives
bearing some familiar glimmer of him,
like a warm faraway breath
briefly fogging the mirror.

Maybe she is keeping her hope for him
alive, as if lying awake for decades,
waiting for his headlights to sweep
across the curtains, the sounds
of his footsteps climbing the stairs,
of his keys settling on the bedside table,
telling her he got home okay, after all,
so she can finally turn off her light
and go to sleep.

Fresh Air

In my childhood climate,
my sister Lynn and our mother
were the main weathermakers.
I learned to watch them
like a meteorologist tracking the isobars
of competing pressure systems,
calculating when it was safe
to relax indoors, maybe having
peanut butter toast and milk
at the kitchen table, and when
to take shelter outside,
playing alone out by the woodpile,
imagining myself living like a hermit
on dogwood berries and puddle water.

The two seemed to me like opposing generals
spoiling for battle—both of them
compact, spirited, energetic, vocal.
I avoided any scene with them
where I might be suddenly called upon
to enlist or hoist a flag of allegiance;

be accused of cowardice;
cause, risk, or witness injury.

So when Lynn moved nearby
to help out with our mother, and
the two mighty forces converged
in the center of my life,
at first, no matter what else
I might be doing or thinking about,
they were always on my mind,
like a tornado watch scrolling
red along the base of a TV screen.
And my body itself,
like the brick stronghold
of the third little pig,
was braced, airtight, defending
against conditions that could
blow my house in.

But inside my barricade,
I also thought, but wait,
how could I hold Lynn at bay,
she who had grown up with me
as if the other half of one complete child?
When we were small, she and I could fit
into a kitchen cabinet next to the pans,
like a couple of still-damp kittens
with their eyes not yet open,
so close in age that even we
couldn't tell ourselves apart.

Our older sister considered me
"the late twin."

But we were not identical.
When Lynn's spirits seemed perilously high,
I kept myself carefully grounded,
like the other shoe in the dull cliché,
the one that must not be allowed to drop.
And when she was down, I tried
to lift her weight, usually in vain,
like a scrawny child flailing helplessly
at the top of a teeter-totter.
We were more symbiotic than alike.

The older we got, the more different
our pasts became, hers and mine.
I came to have the role of the one
my mother had always favored—
maybe like vanilla, her old reliable,
or maybe favored like a weak leg
that could not bear its share of weight.
Lynn became the survivor of battle and insult,
disfavor for her strong will, for being herself.
Yet we played the same game of marbles
from opposite ends of the hallway,
shared the same tub, the same teachers,
the same crayons, bedroom, meals,
brother and sister, back seat, childhood.

Did I wind up with the easy youth
while she, on the see-saw's other end,
got the difficult one? Or even because?
Did I alone have the fun I thought we had?
Did my preference for the sunny side
push her off into the shadows?

Or have all our stories grown too tight for us?
Instead of sprawling textured masterpieces,
have we settled for abridged versions of our lives,
or even summaries with bullet points,
rather than read the whole thing, between the lines?
Have we even closed the book on our narratives
like the slam of a gavel, shutting each other out?

It is a singularly beautiful day, and
here we are, the three characters,
my sister, our mother, and I,
walking into the wind at the park,
past the Civil War monument with its inscriptions
of bloody battles—Vicksburg, Shiloh, Chickamauga—
built in the first relief of an armistice,
Lynn with her hand resting on one side
of our mother's walker, me on the other.

As a child, I might have spent this day alone,
out of earshot, in my outdoor refuge.
Instead, they are with me, as if they had both
crossed the old backyard and all those years
to seek welcome in my private territory—

my fantasy world where all adversaries
could meet for tea and praise me for the cakes
I had made out of mud topped with pebbles.

We look down from the bluff to the river below.
The breeze is troubling the water in a fascinating way,
lighting up fragments that then seem to heal smooth
as the current moves on, like a single body,
under the two bridges and then further west.
The three of us are as silent as the river.

We emerge from shade into natural light.
The park is filled with mature trees, good examples.
In my ribs I feel a doorway blow open,
flooding my body enclosure with fresh air
that seems to pass right through my backbone.
I feel an elated rush of primitive, family hilarity.
I kick aside a fallen branch, a piece of insulation,
pick up some pages that have come loose from a book,
and face a gentle wind that does no harm.

Before and After

From my room I can see my mother's bed vacant.
The safety barricade is no match for her.
Over and over in the night she gets up, gets lost.

Time and again she has to be tucked back in.
She is somewhere out of sight now,
calling and calling my name.
I start to cry, my hands over my face.

After her move to the home for the elderly,
I hear how things are going there:

Over and over in the night she gets up, gets lost.
The safety barricade is no match for her.
Time and again she has to be tucked back in.

From my room I can see my mother's bed vacant.
I start to cry, my hands over my face.
She is somewhere out of sight now,
calling and calling my name.

Mothers and Daughters

At the home for the elderly,
I introduce my 98-year-old mother
to the other residents at the table.
"And I," I announce,
with my hand on my heart,
"am Vivian's mom."
I laugh and quickly correct myself,
but will keep making this mistake.

When we first meet Marie there,
she is tilted back in her recliner.
Her hair is brilliant white, like fiber optics,
her earrings dazzle; her lipstick is fresh and pink.
Catching sight of me, she smiles brightly
and cries: "Why, *hello*!
To think that after all these years,
we would run into one another on a *plane*!"
My mother, standing beside me,
looks on, holding my hand.
Then Marie turns her gaze to her,
exclaiming fondly,
"And my, how you've grown!"

A few days later, this same Marie
is somewhere else again in time—
her beautiful jeweled hand
fluttering in horror over her mouth,
her entire body curled tightly
into the corner of her recliner.
The latest newcomer, June, aged 86,
approaches my mother and me, concerned.

"Do you know where her mother is?"
June asks us, pointing to Marie.
"I think she needs her mother here."
I tell her I don't know.
"I am Vivian's," I explain,
leaving it at that.

June sits down with us, gazing
sympathetically at Marie's distress.
"Actually," she sighs at last, "I don't know
where *my* mother is right now, either."

One day soon after, June is playing rummy
at the table with my mother and me.
Marie, in her recliner, has had a good morning,
singing with some visiting musicians,
clapping her hands in delight.
Now she is napping,
serene as a played-out toddler.

The house is quiet now, peaceful.
I can hear a zipper tinking in the dryer.
There is the smell of dinner cooking.
My mother, June, and I take turns
drawing cards, putting them down.

"Do you have any children, June?" I ask.

"Oh, no," June responds.
"But my daughters do."

After Visiting My Mother

Sometimes there is a feeling
like driving away from the house
where I lived as a child,
having found it painted a chalky blue,
curtained windows looking blank,
the spruce out front missing.
I feel suddenly heavier then,
weighty with responsibility,
this treasure, this freight:

All the scenes that I remember
are nowhere in the world now

but me.

Beyond Belief: The Churchgoer

My mother was born in the parsonage
of a small South Dakota church
where her grandfather served as pastor.
She was raised in her parents' congregation,
even playing piano as a teenager
for the hymns on Sunday mornings.
This was always hard for me to imagine.

Some eighty years later, during a service
of special music at the National Cathedral,
when the congregation knelt for prayer,
my mother remained seated in her chair
with her chin up and spine straight,
loudly declaring, in answer to my glance,
"I don't kneel to ANYBODY."

Unlike most of the children in our school,
we did not attend or belong to anything.
My mother led us nightly in the Lord's Prayer,
but also admonished us not to bother God
by making personal, selfish requests.

When I was curious about the Bible,
she told me it was not suitable reading.

She regularly held forth on the absurdity
of religious practices and beliefs—
Catholic priests in their skirts and petticoats,
Methodists always standing up for this and that,
Baptists dunking one another in bed sheets—
"So much pointless ritual!" she would sigh,
"when the Golden Rule is really all we need."

And the intolerance of all these so-called
Christians she could scarcely believe!
As for "that little wedding cake groom of a man,"
the minister at my sister's church, who dragged a cross
up the aisle during an Easter morning service,
she thought that he had missed his calling—
clearly he hankered after a life in the theater.

Communion, crucifixes, confessions, creeds
all provoked her, and monstrous church buildings
repelled her as the heights of hypocrisy—
people paying for stained-glass windows
instead of schools, so that the poor and uneducated
would stay poor and uneducated from age to age.
"Just look at the history of Latin America," she said.

Yet after my father died, she went to church
with friends, "for the social," as she put it.
She always wore a skirt, nice blouse, and hose;

she could not for the life of her understand
how anyone would show up in dungarees.
"Even during the thirties, when people had nothing,
they would still dress up as best they could."

As for God, she told me not that
she did not believe in Him,
but that she did not think He loved her.
"If He loved me," she declared flatly,
"He wouldn't have made me a widow."
"Do you think that God did that to you?"
I asked. "*You* tell *me*," she replied.

I must have made an unconvincing answer.
Now she is ninety-nine years old; soon enough
she will get whatever chance there turns out to be
to pick that bone with her maker.
But if on that last day she recovers her powers
for argument, I hope that she will find no cause,
not because religion suddenly all makes sense,

but because what she had found so wanting
in theological explanations, in churches,
in society, in the unfairness of disease
and catastrophe, in us, and in her life—
the love itself—is all there for her, not only
what she was missing, but unimaginably more,
beyond what she could ever have believed.

Today

I know that there will be an ending,
but not today.

Today we are walking together along the river.

These crocuses, which in some future spring
will come up without her, are blooming purple today.

I have tied the plaid-lined hood of her red jacket
against the tart wind, for although she, and I, too,
will be cold one day, today we are keeping warm.

We pause on a bench to watch the ducks.
When I put my right hand atop her left,
she stacks her right over mine, expectantly;
she knows what I will do next.
One day nothing will happen next,
but today I clap my left hand atop the stack,
and she pulls her bottom hand out to top mine.

We continue on our way; the wheels of her walker,
collecting damp bits of fallen leaves,
spin like miniature wreaths down the sidewalk.
This is her hundredth twenty-seventh of March.
It is late in the afternoon; her long shadow
stretches east, as if trying hard to pull free.
But the darkness holds off; we do not rush

today.

What Goes Without Saying

I have never told my mother
that we sold her red Toyota and her house,
or that my father's last little brother died.

I have never said anything
about the stroke
that befell my sister's husband,
or the shrinking of the glaciers
in our favorite parks,
or the tornado that leveled
a day care center just two blocks south.

I never mentioned it
when I started paying her bills
and balancing her checkbook,
nor did I make plain to her
how she had wandered our house
in the wee hours, calling and calling me,
such that after my shoulder surgeries,
when I was on painkillers
trying to sleep in the recliner,
I came to dread the sound

of my name.
I never pointed out to her
how she was changing, or named
her diagnosis, or its prognosis,
or the reason for her move
to a home for the elderly.

I have told her that we love her, and we do,
that she has been the best mom, and she has,
but I have never said to her face

how much I miss my mother.

Mom's Birthday Surprise

"Strange, isn't it? Each man's life touches so many other lives."
— Clarence the angel, *It's a Wonderful Life*

On our mother's hundredth birthday,
my brother and sisters and I are gathered together
at my kitchen table, having coffee—a singular event.
In the thirty-nine years since our father's death,
the family has reunited only three times,
that second meeting already thirteen years ago.
In a few hours we will fetch the birthday girl
for cake and ice cream and presents.

But then my cell phone rings,
displaying the name of the elderly home:
our mother is feverish and vomiting.
My sister and I drive down to the place,
bundle her up, and take her to the doctor,
armed with a plastic tub and towels.
She smiles miserably during the exam.
I fill out medical forms with today's date
and our mother's birthdate identical: 1/15/19.

The doctor says it looks like a norovirus,
prescribes medicines to stave off dehydration.

The next night, all the fellow residents,
including the frail woman on oxygen, are sick,
while my sister-in-law and sister, too,
battle nausea in their respective bathrooms.
From my mother the virus spreads to twelve others,
as if she had been a time bomb
set to detonate at exactly the century mark.

Everyone quickly disperses, goes back home.
We throw out the chocolate cake my sister made.
I cancel the weekend party at the Elks Lodge.
Then I wipe down everything with Lysol,
launder bedding, rugs, and towels in hot water.

My mother recovers, and one by one,
so do all the others. The presents wait.
I hope that, before long, we will sing
happy birthday to my mother
in her sparkly new tiara, and that
she will blow out her centenary candle
with one great wishing breath—
but nobody yet has the stomach for it.

Dementia and/or My Mother

It is a sunny lunchtime.
I am sitting beside my mother,
offering her a teaspoon
of strawberry yogurt.
Her lips open,
but her eyes are blank.

Today, though, that blankness
where the person used to be
freezes me with terror.
The force that has destroyed
my mother's mind and
taken so much of her life
wants more. It is not inert.
It is hungry.

With the spoon in my hand,
I hesitate: what if
I have been nurturing
not my mother, but
this?—this destroyer
of her conscious life?—

feeding and feeding it
with my own years, too,
my health, and attention,
even this yogurt now—
empowering it so that
it can victimize her,
consume me,
and steal time
from my newborn grandson?

It seems to wait
with its mouth open,
the entrance to a moist black cave
where a monster thrives
and the river of Lethe
carves and carves.

The Citizen

As a child, I would watch my mother
at the typewriter, her fingers a blur,
her face a marvel of conviction,
as she informed her congressman
how he ought to vote, or persuaded him
to take a more enlightened view of things.
Even after I was married and lived out of state,
upon learning that we had had to pay
for her grandsons' required school textbooks,
she complained to our elected representatives.

She wrote letters to the editor
denouncing the use of sexy images
to sell publications, condemned
the idea that celebrities' lives were "news,"
and deplored the increasing ratio
of advertising to factual reporting.
She sent notice when she cancelled
subscriptions on ethical grounds.

When my sister was in eighth grade
and was scheduled to take a class trip

to see *Romeo and Juliet*, rated "M,"
my mother refused to sign the permission slip,
deeming it wrong for a young actress
to have to bare her breasts for a movie,
and wrong for a public school to support
the film industry's exploitation of women,
and wrong for families to be pressured into paying
for their children's entertainment as part of
what was supposed to be universal free education.
My sister had to stay behind at school that day,
doing nothing but—understandably—fuming.

When the white girl across the street
called their maid, an African American woman,
by her first name, and I mentioned this in passing,
my mother caught me by the collar
and told me that never
ever should a child
refer to any grown-up
by her first name, and if I did not know
Miss or Mrs. *What* (as I protested),
it was my own responsibility
to find out what to call her
to show her the respect that she deserved.

We had two daily papers delivered,
morning and evening, and she read both.
She watched news on all the networks,
switching the channel selector back and forth
(or using the pliers during that period

when the knob would not stay on),
noting which stories were featured,
the language and tone used by the anchors,
detecting and judging their biases.
She watched the Fulbright hearings,
the Watergate hearings, the testimony
of Anita Hill, the Iran-Contra affair.
She read the Warren Report cover to cover.
When my brother was in Vietnam
the TV was almost perpetually on,
in case of bulletins, and she knew
how every member of Congress
stood, or avoided making a stand,
on the subject of the war.

She knew that policies and world events
could reach right into people's houses
and take the food from their tables,
press their children into service,
imprison truthtellers, bankrupt,
kill and destroy, force families to flee.
For her, citizenship was an activity
to be engaged in strenuously every day,
a fight for life, not just a set of perks.

When my mother became a widow,
she began walking the mile
up to the main road and back
each morning, carrying a trowel
and a plastic bag to collect litter.

She kept that section of roadway
clean for thirty years, even when
it was scary to watch her at ninety,
scrambling over a guardrail to collect
that empty bottle of vodka she knew
would be down in the creek bed, where
it was regularly thrown out a car window
by someone probably living in one
of the mansions that had cropped up
along her once rustic country road,
whose secret alcoholism troubled her.
There was never a day, she said, without new trash.

Even after she could not see well enough
to file a ballot, she voted, appointing me to read
aloud the candidates' names, the referenda.
Even then, my mother kept up with the news.
She would stand two feet in front of the TV
and punch the power button of the remote, hard,
saying, "Better see what the rascals have been up to."
And when the dementia and macular degeneration
and deafness were starting to wall her in,
she made one last outcry for Trayvon Martin.
She spoke of the shooting over and over on the phone—
could not get him out of her head, she said—
how upset she was by the racism and injustice,
by what it revealed about us as a country,
by how far it showed we had not come.
As always, she felt personally responsible.

Of all the times that I miss my mother
when I am with my mother, these moments
when she would have been most outraged,
most vocal, most provoked in conscience and wit,
and yet now sits passively, looking on in silence
while all she had put her heart into as a citizen
comes under attack—her sword, her pen,
her very self asleep—I believe I miss her most.

Memory Loss

Standing on a chair in my closet,
I take the lid from a cardboard box.
Out gusts the forgotten smell
of my mother's old dresser drawers.

I inhale the once-familiar atmosphere
like an astronaut returned from outer space,
when he opens the tight hatch of the capsule
and takes again an earthling breath of air.

It had a tonic quality, my mother's life—
something like the faint mineral smell
that rises from the rapids of a rocky stream
during a spring snowmelt in the mountains.

It was an ambience neither good nor bad—
just as a stone or a tree is neither good nor bad;
and when it reaches my lungs, I remember
my life when it was neither good nor bad.

The little whiff contains trace elements
of my whole childhood habitat—the back steps,

library books fringed with torn bits of paper,
the broom and mop standing in the corner,
the heating vent in the kneehole of the yellow desk,
where I would lie on the rug and warm my sock feet,
the soup cans on the kitchen cupboard shelf,
that little jar of marbles, the white and orange one
with the nicked surface that would not roll straight;
and always music—Chopin or Scott Joplin,
Flatt and Scruggs or Ian and Sylvia,
South Pacific or the Beatles or Herb Alpert,
from the piano, television, clock radios,
or just from voices moving room to room.

The stored box turns out to contain
my mother's perfect strand of pearls,
brought home from Japan by my father,
a few scarves, a handmade bookmark,
and my own braids, cut off on the last day
of elementary school—my own ceremony
for ending childhood forever.
But I clap the lid back on quickly,
so as to recapture the precious molecules,
the feeling of what it was like to be me.

When I climbed up to reach the box,
I had been in a ruthlessly efficient mood,
seeking to eliminate clutter, distress,
as if to throw out the bathwater without looking.

But when I step down from the chair,
I no longer want to clear my life of its life.
My mother's memory loss took her from herself,
yes, but I cannot let it take her also from me—

for in forgetting her, I, too, would vanish.

A Fantasy of La-la Land

"Enough already!" my mother exclaims at last.
Flinging the blanket from her lap,
she stands up from the recliner so abruptly
that it rocks on violently, alone.
"That Alzheimer's was the *pits*!"
She pries the hearing aid from each ear,
then stands motionless a moment.
"Why, I don't think I have heard
a bird sing like that in twenty years."
Suddenly gripping her bare wrist,
she asks, "What did I do with my watch?
I've lost all track of time."
She takes a couple steps toward the kitchen
to read, from afar, the clock on the stove.
"Better turn on the news and see
what country we've blown up
while I've been sitting there on my duff."
I find the TV remote. She continues,
"I bet I have a stack of unanswered letters
yay high" (she draws a flat hand across
her forehead). "I'll have to buy new stamps;
they probably cost an arm and a leg now."

She sits down in front of the set, then asks,
"Where is Gwen Ifill? I see they have
a new dame on with Judy Woodruff."
While current events unfold on the screen,
she shakes her head: "Good Lord!
The lunatics are running the asylum!"
Then as the closing credits roll,
she glances down at herself, grimacing.
"How long have I been slopping around
in these God-awful clothes?
Your dad would be absolutely appalled!"
Finally she turns a level look at me.
"Well, girl, what's the scuttlebutt?
What have you been up to
while I've been off in La-La Land?"

Her Childbearing Years

Sometimes I wonder if
my mother is waiting
for us all to get over it—
"it" being our upbringing,
which left us confident
that we will never be good
at getting over anything.

She trained us to recognize
that even the first straw
could well be one
that breaks the camel's back:
so better be wary—
better not take anything on.

If you get a dog, for example,
you have just doomed yourself,
first to worry that one day
it will snap its leash on you,
and then to heartache when it dies.

You couldn't endure the suffering.

Also, the seeds of calamity can be small,
so whenever anything bad does happen,
sift through everything afterward
minutely, until you can find a way
that you could have made things otherwise.
Never give up looking for the black box
that will prove that you did something wrong.

So maybe my mother is just trying to last,
bearing up now for a hundred years
so that her children don't have to bear
what we would find unbearable—
what she knows (and it's true)
we could never get over.

Cruelty

This morning the president
of the college women's athletics club
for the 1937-38 academic year
is hoisted from her bed
with a mechanical lift.

She who skipped a grade
and won all the spelling bees
is found with a hearing aid
tucked inside her cheek.

She who kept four file boxes
of recipe cards speckled with sauces,
handwriting luminous with grease,
forgets at lunch how to swallow
a mouthful of pureed goulash.

Now this afternoon I push her wheelchair
through the gardens of the nursing home,
her expression as blank as that
of the elderly woman we once saw

thirty years ago, when
she turned to me
with an anguished expression
and said, "Oh, Jan,
I hope to God
I never get like that."

Cruelty II

Have I demanded
that she stay the same,
when she can't?

Have I shown her
my disappointment
when she does not know me?
Do I display my fright
when she chokes on a sip of water?
When she cannot stand up,
is it panic she reads on my face?

Is she living in a world now
where everyone around her
looks disturbed to see her—
as another physical chore,
an unsolved medical case,
a human tragedy,
a failure in the eyes of those
who look most familiar?

Please let me accept her
as she is—now—
without insisting
that she perform her old tricks,
or that she show me signs
of a personality
she no longer has.

Please let me communicate
a reliable softness,
a grateful assurance
that she has already been
and done
and given
enough,
and more than enough.

The Inadequacies of Pig Latin

My mother's tongue was sharp,
but clean. She could not abide
vulgarity.

One summer,
driving in a hard rain
on his sole vacation of the year,
watching the left rear hubcap
that had just popped off
our new rotary engine Mazda
twirl and zag
into oncoming traffic,
my father was heard to mutter,
"Shit!"—
but my mother never did,
not even once.

Now the wheels
have come off her life.

Who can respond for her,
now that he is gone,
and her own mouth
has been buttoned up
the rest of the way?

Surely the situation deserves the worst curse
she would ever have allowed herself,
but it makes me smile, alas, to say it:

Amn-day.

Envoy

I used to believe that the Viking burial ships—
Sutton Hoo, and Scandinavian stone boats—
had actually set sail with the honored dead,
bearing their caches of treasure out to sea,
where they would drift to another shore or sink
in a whale road saga that none alive would know.
The soul, richly equipped, would make its passage,
and the vessel with its gold and filigreed swords,
silver bowls, bones, and hasps of figured metal
would be discovered by future strangers
like a coded message in a bottle, to be read:
This person was someone special.

But the funerary ships that carried the dead
were laid in the earth, not set forth on the sea,
so those ancient sorrowers stood on the dirt,
as we will stand, beside their lost treasure,
watching the gold and silver going nowhere.
Who was it they wanted to reach eternity?

I have been urged to prearrange
my mother's funeral. I must see to it.

Long distance transportation will be required.
She wished to be buried with my father,
with the letters he had written to her in wartime,
hopeful love letters that she treasured all her life.

Death is coming to spirit off all that remains:
each time she swirled meringue
atop a lemon pie, sealing it to the edges,
or put on her yellow suit and heels
and walked the path to school
for parent-teacher conference day,
or stood in the drugstore aisle
choosing a "thoughty" birthday card,
or drew a strand of tinsel across a branch
after midnight on a Christmas Eve,
or drizzled hot divinity from a spoon
and groped in the cold water for a glob
to crack against the side of the cup,
or wrote a letter and walked it down to the mailbox,
or spoke up against cruelty or injustice or ignorance,
or traveled cross country days and nights
on a Greyhound bus to see her grandchildren;

surely everything she got a real kick out of, too—
mastering "Kitten on the Keys" on the piano,
reading and rereading Thackeray's *Vanity Fair*,
listening to Hot Jazz Saturday Night on the radio,
watching the Baltimore Orioles play on TV
while doing the daily crossword,

dancing in the kitchen along with the fiddler
on the Porter Waggoner show,
riding in the Chrysler while my dad drove,
picking up a spare at duckpins,
stooping to pick up a gleaming rock
from a rocky mountain stream;

all the good she did, as well, that went unnoticed—
like a sleep that nourishes, or rain that falls by night—
and the vitality that her life germinated in others,
and all that she offered but was not received—
when she knocked at one or another hard-shut heart,
holding a gift—all those intended transactions
are now complete, fulfilled, beautiful, imperishable;

nothing, though, that was wrought by fatigue,
fear, haste, frustration, envy, anxiety,
inattention, or just insufficient light—
unconscious harm never having been
what her spirit truly meant,
and thus no more real or lasting
than a savage punch thrown in the nightmare
of a child, who forgets it at sunrise;
and in turn, no injury that she ever suffered
from our own unmindful thrashings—
no residual pain, no insoluble vexation.

Dementia has been picking at my mother's brain
like crows pulling with their beaks

at a bloody animal in the road.
Her dying is gruesome, unpoetic, long.
But death is not the subject of my mother's life.
While moths, say, can devour a familiar green sweater,
they cannot touch the afternoons when it was worn,
the shared human feeling, the scent of past autumns,
the warmth it gave, or even what happens to us now
when it reappears in an old photograph or dream.

And the memories that my mother herself treasured
before her mind was ransacked cannot stay lost;
she will reach into the mailbox with a little girl's hand
and retrieve the birthday card from her grandmother.

I don't want to say goodbye, but it may be time
to wend toward the dock with my handkerchief,
to see off the treasure ship with its invisible goods.
I hope my mother feels that her vessel is light,
and yet that her life entire has been saved—
every single thing her heart ever had a hand in,
known or unknown to anyone else,
forgotten or unforgotten to herself—
but nothing else at all, no added weight,
no guilt, no nagging thing left still undone—
so she can cut loose and sail home
free to the source of her mystery,
the gifts of her spirit received in full.

Meanwhile we can attend the launch at the tumulus
with our familiar muddy shoes, our golden mementoes,
and the same throbbing hearts as our Viking forbears,
our lives at once bereft and brimming over,
calling across the ages, Remember! Treasure! Farewell!

June 3, 2020

The tide had been going out a long time,
exposing, at first, lost pages of sheet music,
recipe cards, a pocket calendar, an address book
with a half sheet of old Forever stamps.
Farther out, a favorite classy blouse, dress shoes,
a wristwatch, a large-print biography, a pen,
a set of keys; beyond that, an upended walker,
a sports bottle with a straw, a red jacket,
a scattered deck of cards, a blue balloon.
And on the damp seabed close to the horizon,
just a littering—a chapstick, a spoon
leaning in a half glass of thickened orange juice,
a catheter, a mangled tube of bedsore ointment.

Any island elder can tell you what it means
when the sea keeps going out and out like this:
a wave is gathering that will overwhelm you.
And so it was that beyond the edge of the world,
beyond the room that my mother was departing,
the whole mass of her fluid and powerful life
had been collecting and building, such that
at 6:38 pm, it all would come racing back in,

refilling and replenishing every moment and object
with that spirit of the fastest little girl in the school,
reanimating the sad and disinhabited spaces
of my memory, revivifying her history—and mine—
toppling me, forcing me, in the wash of gratitude,
all the way back to my old home and childhood,
with its kitchens and cars and sofas and gardens,
then setting me down as tenderly as a mother
telling her child good night, good night.

A Time and Place to Mourn

If the house were still standing
I could drive back there—
my car would remember the way—
crunching up the gravel drive,
startling birds from the apple trees.
I would find the muddy key
under the brick by the first fencepost,
push open the Dutch door
and let myself into the empty house,
into a gust of its particular smell.
I would pass through the kitchen
where the red-rimmed clock
would still be ticking over the sink,
and run my fingers over the counter
through the crumbs by the toaster.
I would approach the fireplace,
the green corduroy chair,
the red hassock strewn with newspapers,
then turn to mount the stairs,
my feet thudding softly
on the thick wool carpet,
my face lit from above

by the bathroom window.
At the landing I would bear right,
past the hamper and the portrait of our cat,
painted by my sister when she was fourteen,
and into my room with its corner windows.
Above the bureau, the mirror that reflected me
at four years of age would briefly show me now.
I would lie down on my low twin bed
with its blue quilt, under the bulletin board
with the satellite photos of the moon
that my dad once brought home from work.
Across the landing their double bed would be made,
the sadiron I had found by a creek in the Yukon
propping the door open, as usual, so it does not slam.
After a while, maybe I would notice from outdoors
the scent of the wild grapes that used to grow
along the clear little stream on the east side,
back when it still ran, whether in wet times or dry.
And that will do, to cry for my mother at last.

My Travel Companion

Even when my mother could no longer
remember my name, she remained
uncannily proficient on road trips,
flipping the visor down reflexively
when we drove west into the sun.

She and my dad raised us to travel in cars,
to read and refold maps, to avoid big city traffic,
to take the dotted lines of scenic routes.
The highway was transcendent for us children,
leading us beyond ourselves, bringing us home.

As adults, we still craved long drives,
unpeopled landscapes, little cafes, faraway kin.
After our father died, Mom would come along
in our own backseats, next to a child or two.
"Just let me grab my toothbrush!" she would say.

In the early years of her dementia, she and I still
would go, and she stopped caring where.
I began adding tangents of personal curiosity

to our trips to the White Mountains, the Gulf Coast,
the Smokies, the Hudson Valley, the Black Hills.

There is a photo of her in a pretty blouse
sweating by the roses outside Helen Keller's home
in Tuscumbia, near the pump whose water
reconnected the little girl to language,
where she learned to spell into a human hand.

In Concord, while our tour guide literally bit her lip,
my mother patted the extended window ledge
that served Louisa May Alcott as a desk
when she wrote from the heart of her own life,
in an upstairs bedroom shared with her sister.

In Chadds Ford, I held my mother's hand
as we walked between the house and the studio
of N. C. Wyeth, along a little footpath,
which was all the separation he had wanted
between his work and his family.

In Plains we visited the Carters' small church
and the historic farm site, where my mother halted
before what looked like a peculiar stationary bike—
a pedal-operated grinding stone for sharpening tools,
which brought her father back to a cleared mind.

We saw W. C. Handy's piano, the boarding house
where Thomas Wolfe was raised, the street in Mankato
where Maud Hart Lovelace imagined Betsy and Tacy—

each life stemming from its own place and people,
bearing original fruit from original roots.

As we rode from birthplace to birthplace,
wherever we went, I searched for local places
offering fried scallops—my mother's favorite—
lemon meringue pie, liver and onions,
a good waffle, food served on real plates.

At night we would play Scrabble
in our motel room, drinking Cokes
with a little splash of bourbon apiece.
We would set out early with our coffee,
when the sun was magic on the fields.

Now my empty passenger seat looks
expectant, ready for a jaunt—as if
her eagerness to go survived her,
and my origins accompany me still.
I feel perpetually lit, like a motel with a vacancy.

In Closing

These poems were made with words she gave to me,
with typing learned on her Remington Rand,
with her cadences, which come naturally,
like the dialect of one's native land.
I have tried here to be brave, clear, exact,
to scorn, as she would do, glib sentiments,
to trust that, sweet or bitter, any fact
tastes more like life than would false innocence.
Yet she would not have written poems like these,
nor likely chosen this book from a shelf,
and were her mind not blunted by disease,
I doubt I'd ever so expose myself.
But reader, I have felt compelled, because
how else now can you know her as she was?

The author and her mother, Vivian Frame, 1956

Printed in the USA
CPSIA information can be obtained
at www.ICGtesting.com
LVHW051447290524
781286LV00002B/368